SECTION 1: INTRODUCTION TO NUMBERS

I have __1__ apple

one

Let's write 1

I have 2 cars

two

1 2 3 4 5 6 7 8 9 10 11 12 13 14 15 16 17 18 19 20

Let's write 2

2 2 2 2 2 2 2 2

I have 3 cakes

three

1 2 3 4 5 6 7 8 9 10 11 12 13 14 15 16 17 18 19 20

Let's write 3

3 3 3 3 3 3 3 3

I have 4 frogs

four

Let's write 4

I have 5 houses

five

Let's write 5

5 5 5 5 5 5 5 5

1 2 3 4 5 6 7 8 9 10 11 12 13 14 15 16 17 18 19 20

I have 6 phones

six

Let's write 6

6 6 6 6 6 6 6 6

1 2 3 4 5 6 7 8 9 10 11 12 13 14 15 16 17 18 19 20

I have 7 chairs

seven

Let's write 7

7 7 7 7 7 7 7 7 7

I have 8 lions

eight

Let's write 8

8 8 8 8 8 8 8 8

I have 9 pens

nine

Let's write q

I have 10 clocks

ten

1 2 3 4 5 6 7 8 9 10 11 12 13 14 15 16 17 18 19 20

Let's write 10

10 10 10 10 10 10 10

I have 11 crabs

eleven

Let's write 11

I have 12 pots

twelve

Let's write 12

I have 13 hats

thirteen

1 2 3 4 5 6 7 8 9 10 11 12 13 14 15 16 17 18 19 20

Let's write 13

13 13 13 13 13 13 13 13

I have 14 balloons

fourteen

1 2 3 4 5 6 7 8 9 10 11 12 13 14 15 16 17 18 19 20

Let's write 14

I have 15 watches

fifteen

Let's write 15

I have 16 drums

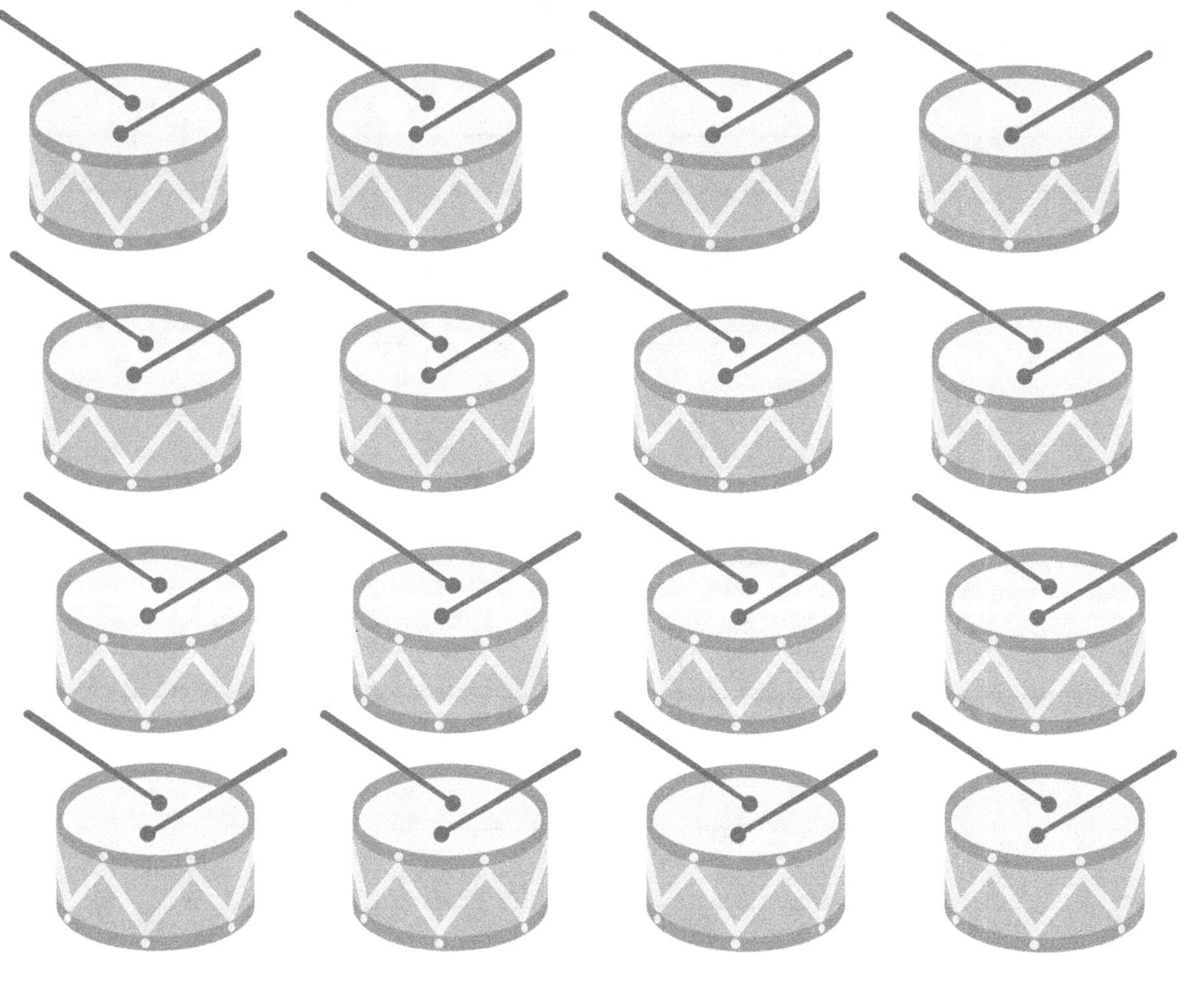

sixteen

1 2 3 4 5 6 7 8 9 10 11 12 13 14 15 16 17 18 19 20

Let's write 16

16 16 16 16 16 16 16

I have 17 trees

seventeen

1 2 3 4 5 6 7 8 9 10 11 12 13 14 15 16 17 18 19 20

Let's write 17

17 17 17 17 17 17 17 17

1 2 3 4 5 6 7 8 9 10 11 12 13 14 15 16 17 18 19 20

I have 18 cats

eighteen

1 2 3 4 5 6 7 8 9 10 11 12 13 14 15 16 17 18 19 20

Let's write 18

18 18 18 18 18 18 18 18

I have 19 fish

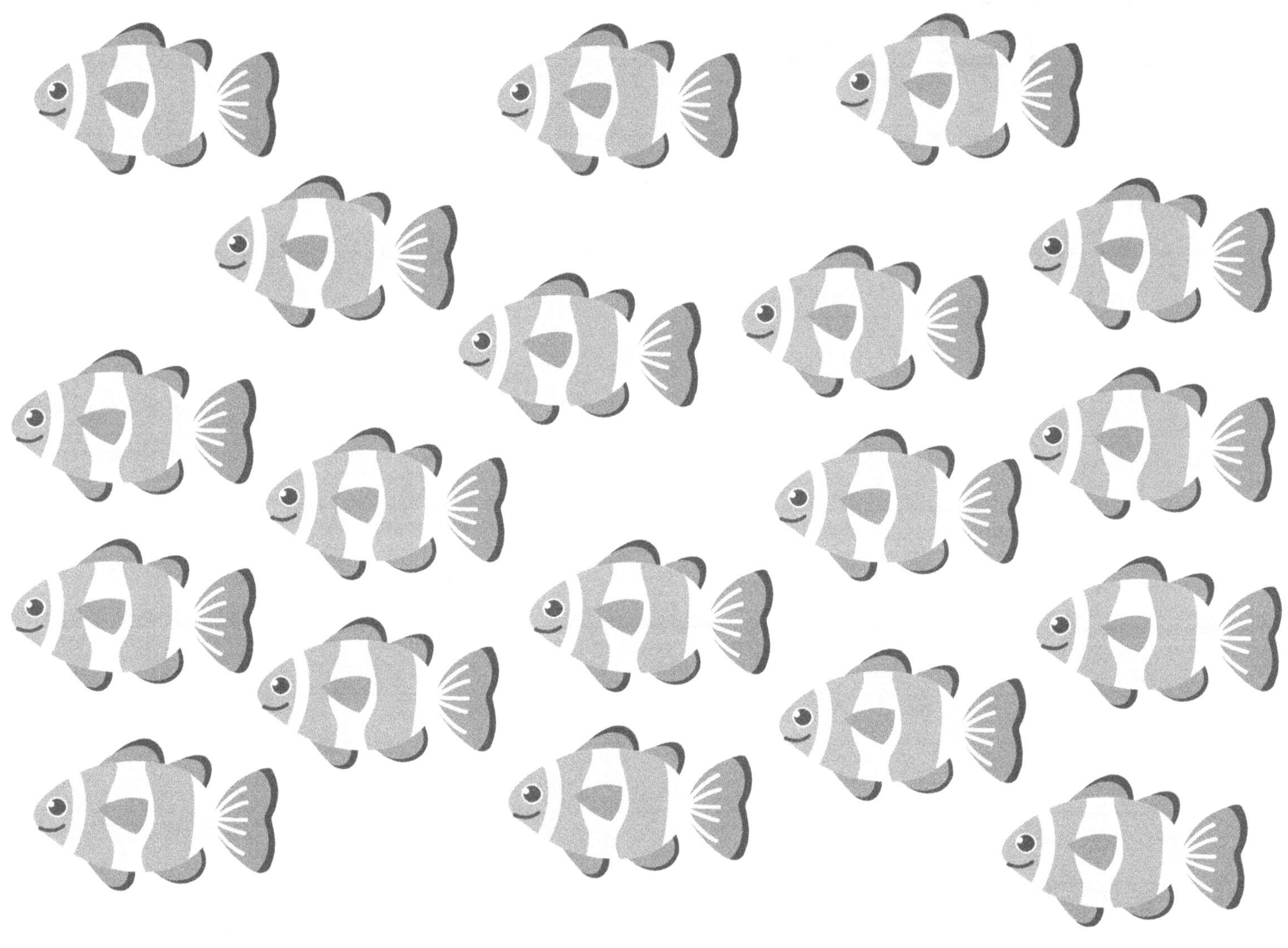

nineteen

Let's write 19

1 2 3 4 5 6 7 8 9 10 11 12 13 14 15 16 17 18 19 20

I have 20 boats

twenty

1 2 3 4 5 6 7 8 9 10 11 12 13 14 15 16 17 18 19 20

Let's write 20

20 20 20 20 20 20

GREAT JOB SO FAR!

NOW YOU KNOW YOUR NUMBERS!

SECTION 2: LET'S LEARN ADDITION

Addition is when we take two or more numbers and put them together to make a new total

$$2 + 1 = 3$$

Above, 2 stars are added to 1 other star to make a total of 3 stars

Let's see a few more examples . . .

$$3 + 1 = 4$$

$$1 + 2 = 3$$

$$2 + 3 = 5$$

LET'S LEARN ADDITION

4 + 1 = 5

3 + 6 = 9

Now your turn 

LET'S LEARN
ADDITION

1 + 1 = ☐

1 + 2 = ☐

2 + 3 = ☐

LET'S LEARN
ADDITION

4 + 2 = ☐

3 + 3 = ☐

2 + 2 = ☐

Let's take away the stars

1 + 2 =

1 + 4 =

2 + 3 =

ADDITION

Let's take away the stars

5 + 3 = ☐

4 + 5 = ☐

4 + 4 = ☐

LET'S LEARN
ADDITION

Sums can also look like this:

$$6 + 5 =$$

$$5 + 3 =$$

$$7 + 2 =$$

$$5 + 4 =$$

ADDITION

Sums can also look like this:

$$\begin{array}{r} 3 \\ +3 \\ \hline \end{array} \qquad \begin{array}{r} 9 \\ +0 \\ \hline \end{array}$$

$$\begin{array}{r} 6 \\ +3 \\ \hline \end{array} \qquad \begin{array}{r} 7 \\ +1 \\ \hline \end{array}$$

SECTION 3: ADDITION IN ACTION

ADDITION IN ACTION

Count the circles, write down the numbers, solve the sum

1)
$$\begin{array}{r} 4 \\ + 1 \\ \hline 5 \end{array}$$

2)
$$\begin{array}{r} \square \\ + \square \\ \hline \end{array}$$

3)
$$\begin{array}{r} \square \\ + \square \\ \hline \end{array}$$

4)
$$\begin{array}{r} \square \\ + \square \\ \hline \end{array}$$

5)
$$\begin{array}{r} \square \\ + \square \\ \hline \end{array}$$

6)
$$\begin{array}{r} \square \\ + \square \\ \hline \end{array}$$

7)
$$\begin{array}{r} \square \\ + \square \\ \hline \end{array}$$

8)
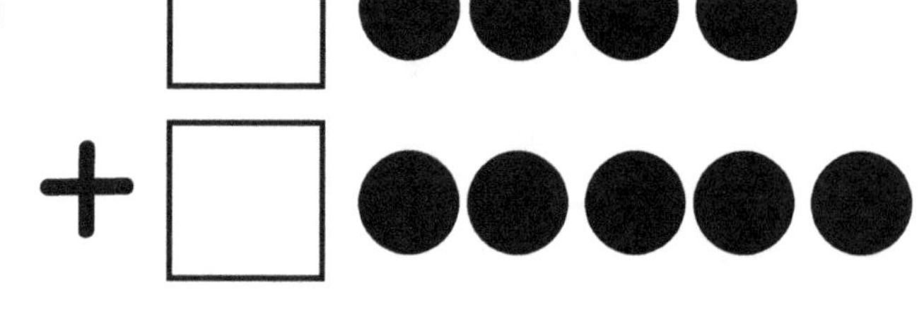

ADDITION IN ACTION

Count the circles, write down the numbers, solve the sum

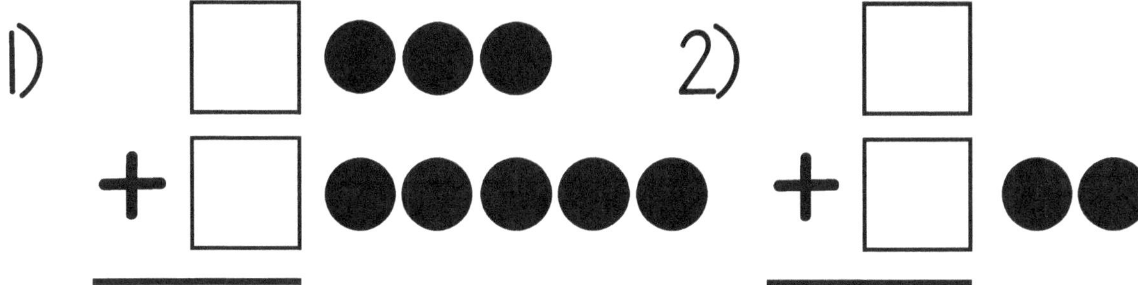

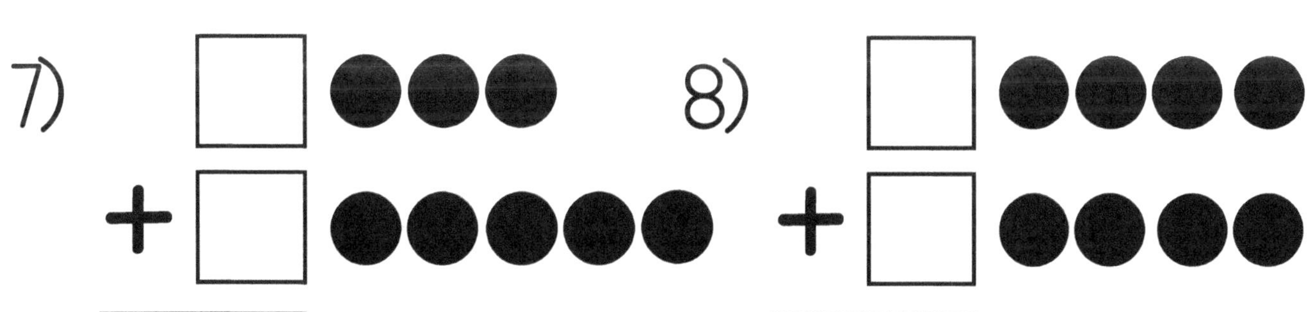

ADDITION IN ACTION

Count the circles, write down the numbers, solve the sum

1) 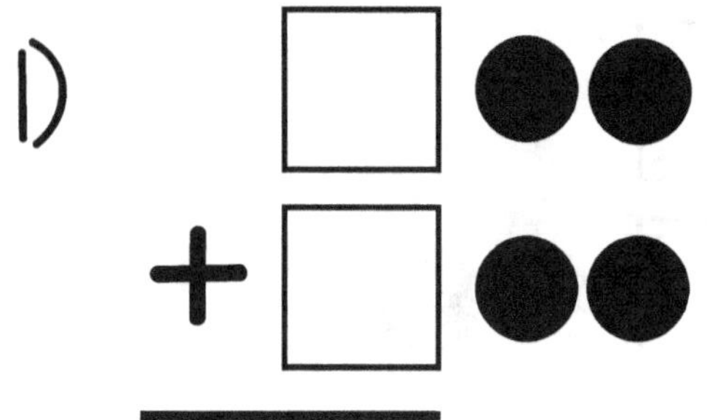

2) 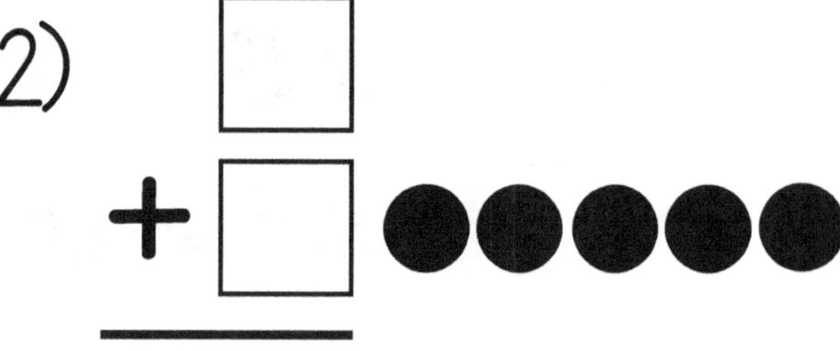

3) 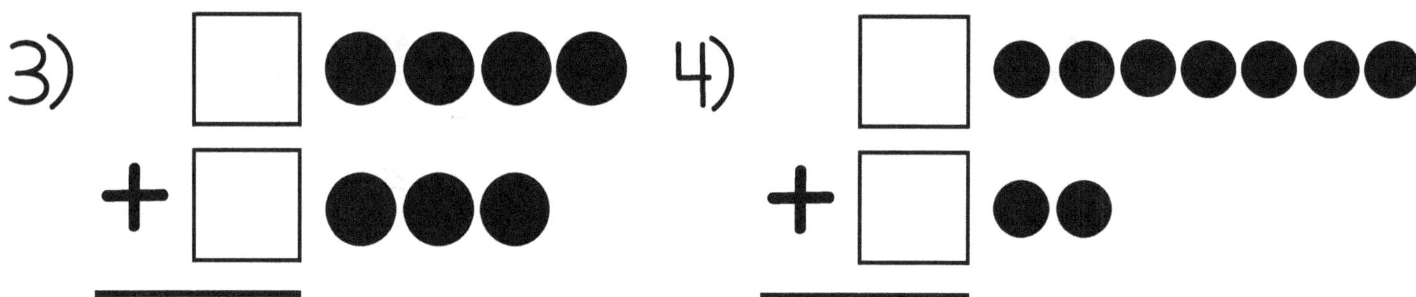

4)

5)

6)

7) 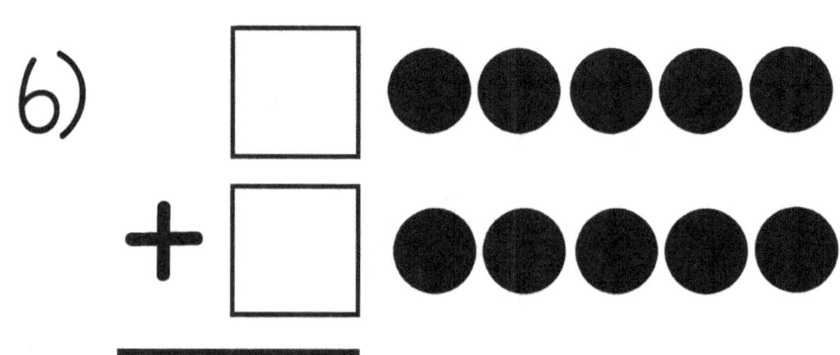

8)

Count the circles, write down the numbers, solve the sum

1) 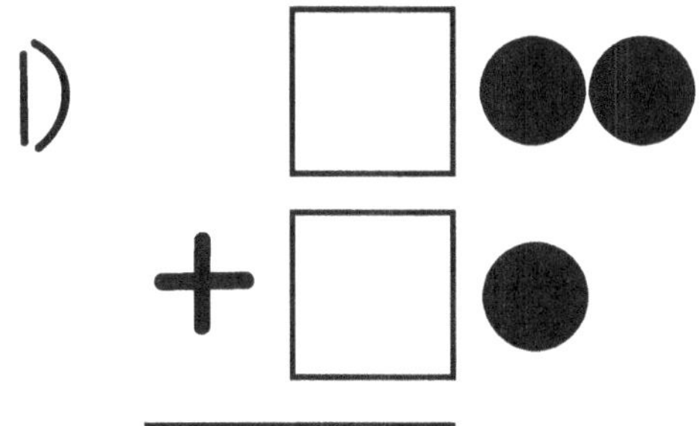

2) 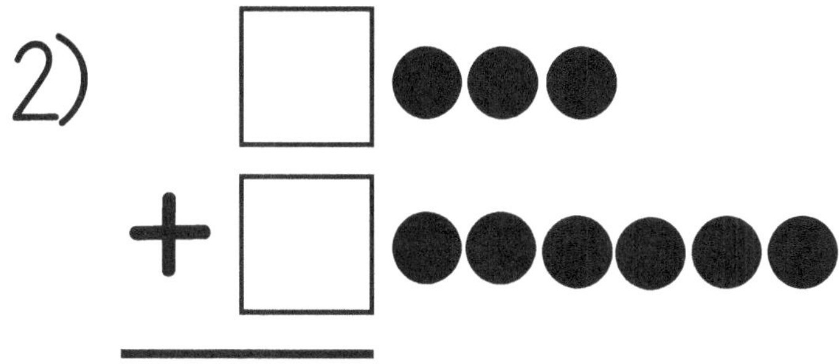

3) 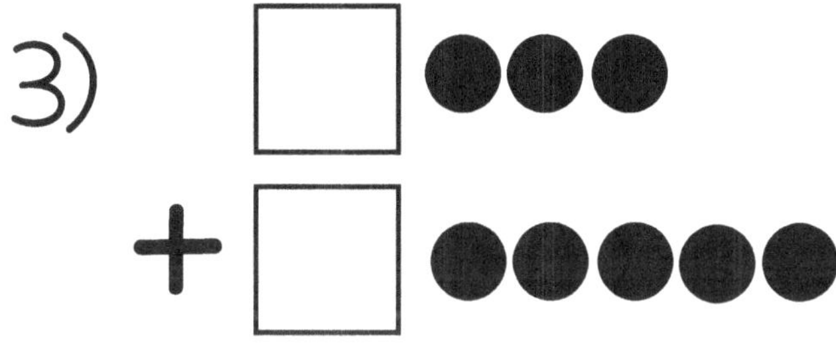

4) 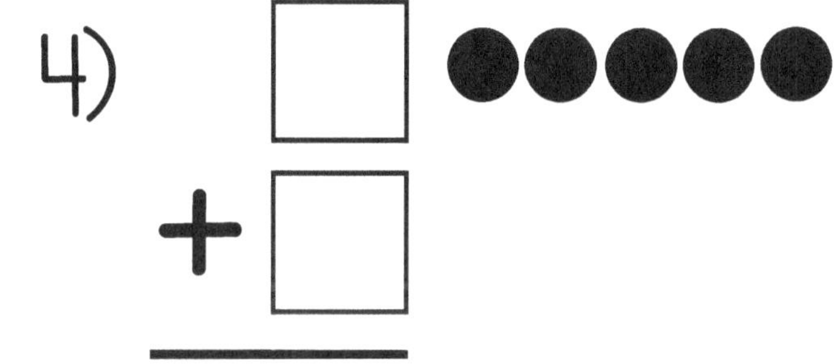

5)

6) 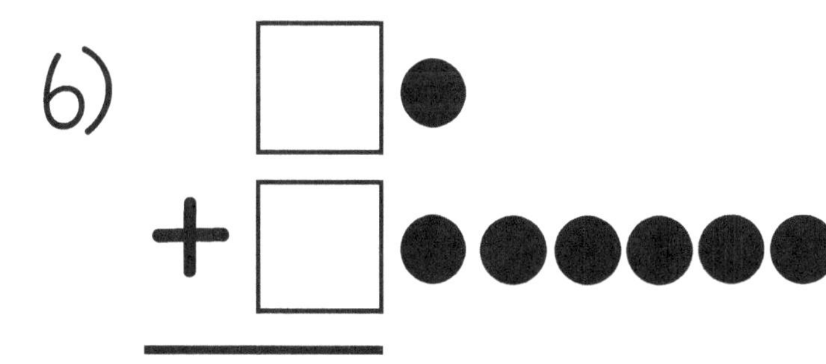

7)

8)

ADDITION IN ACTION

Count the circles, write down the numbers, solve the sum

1)  +  $\underline{1} + \underline{1} = \underline{2}$

2)  $\underline{} + \underline{} = \underline{}$

3) $\underline{} + \underline{} = \underline{}$

4)  $\underline{} + \underline{} = \underline{}$

5)  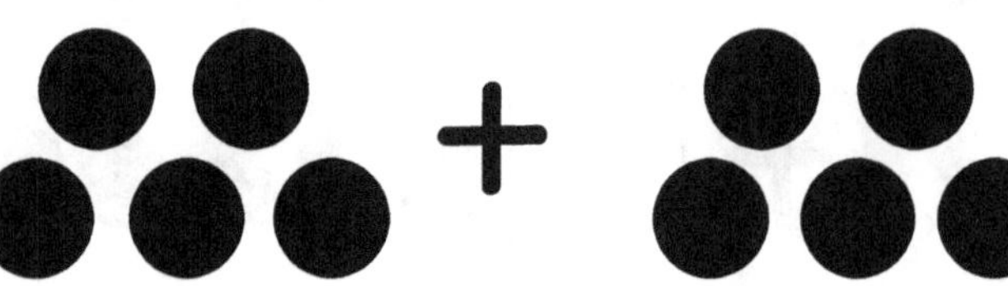 $\underline{} + \underline{} = \underline{}$

ADDITION IN ACTION

Count the circles, write down the numbers, solve the sum

1) _ + _ = _

2) _ + _ = _

3) _ + _ = _

4) _ + _ = _

5) _ + _ = _

ADDITION IN ACTION

Count the circles, write down the numbers, solve the sum

1) _ + _ = _

2) _ + _ = _

3) _ + _ = _

4) _ + _ = _

5) _ + _ = _

ADDITION IN ACTION

Count the circles, write down the numbers, solve the sum

1) _ + _ = _

2) _ + _ = _

3) _ + _ = _

4) _ + _ = _

5) _ + _ = _

ADDITION IN ACTION

Draw circles until you reach 10 in total. Write the missing number.

1) $\underline{8} + \underline{2} = \underline{10}$

2) $\underline{} + \underline{6} = \underline{10}$

3) $\underline{} + \underline{4} = \underline{10}$

4) $\underline{} + \underline{9} = \underline{10}$

5) $\underline{} + \underline{3} = \underline{10}$

ADDITION IN ACTION

Draw circles until you reach 10 in total. Write the missing number.

1)   **+**   ○   _ **+** 1 **=** 10

2)   **+** (9 circles)   _ **+** 8 **=** 10

3)   **+** (10 circles)   _ **+** 10 **=** 10

4)   **+** (5 circles)   _ **+** 5 **=** 10

5)   **+** (7 circles)   _ **+** 7 **=** 10

ADDITION IN ACTION

Draw circles until you reach 15 in total. Write the missing number.

1) $+$ ◯◯ $\underline{} + \underline{2} = \underline{15}$

2) $+$ ◯◯◯ ◯◯◯ ◯◯◯ $\underline{} + \underline{9} = \underline{15}$

3) $+$ ◯◯◯ ◯◯◯ ◯◯ $\underline{} + \underline{8} = \underline{15}$

4) $+$ ◯◯◯ ◯ $\underline{} + \underline{4} = \underline{15}$

5) $+$ ◯◯◯ ◯◯◯ $\underline{} + \underline{6} = \underline{15}$

Draw circles until you reach 15 in total. Write the missing number.

1) + OOO   _ + 3 = 15

2) + (9 circles)   _ + 7 = 15

3) + O   _ + 1 = 15

4) + (10 circles)   _ + 10 = 15

5) + (5 circles)   _ + 5 = 15

ADDITION IN ACTION

Add the two numbers to complete the sum

1) $9 + 4 = 13$

2) $8 + 8 =$

3) $8 + 4 =$

4) $7 + 2 =$

5) $1 + 6 =$

6) $6 + 4 =$

7) $1 + 5 =$

8) $2 + 5 =$

9) $4 + 6 =$

10) $3 + 6 =$

11) $3 + 3 =$

12) $2 + 4 =$

Add the two numbers to complete the sum

1) $0 + 4 =$

2) $1 + 0 =$

3) $7 + 3 =$

4) $9 + 0 =$

5) $4 + 7 =$

6) $5 + 9 =$

7) $8 + 7 =$

8) $4 + 5 =$

9) $7 + 8 =$

10) $7 + 4 =$

11) $7 + 7 =$

12) $7 + 6 =$

ADDITION IN ACTION

Add the two numbers to complete the sum

1) $4 + 8 =$

2) $2 + 2 =$

3) $6 + 5 =$

4) $5 + 11 =$

5) $4 + 10 =$

6) $9 + 9 =$

7) $9 + 7 =$

8) $3 + 11 =$

9) $4 + 12 =$

10) $8 + 10 =$

11) $6 + 7 =$

12) $13 + 4 =$

Add the two numbers to complete the sum

1) $4 + 14 =$

2) $2 + 12 =$

3) $3 + 15 =$

4) $3 + 17 =$

5) $0 + 19 =$

6) $4 + 13 =$

7) $3 + 16 =$

8) $2 + 17 =$

9) $1 + 19 =$

10) $5 + 14 =$

11) $8 + 12 =$

12) $0 + 20 =$

ADDITION IN ACTION

Write the missing number to make the sum complete

1) $\_ + 2 = 6$ 2) $\_ + 3 = 7$

3) $\_ + 1 = 7$ 4) $\_ + 1 = 9$

5) $\_ + 2 = 9$ 6) $\_ + 6 = 9$

7) $\_ + 3 = 6$ 8) $\_ + 3 = 8$

9) $\_ + 5 = 10$ 10) $\_ + 7 = 10$

11) $\_ + 8 = 10$ 12) $\_ + 2 = 7$

ADDITION IN ACTION

Write the missing number to make the sum complete

1) __ + 3 = 10   2) __ + 7 = 11

3) __ + 2 = 11   4) __ + 4 = 10

5) __ + 7 = 12   6) __ + 2 = 14

7) __ + 6 = 12   8) __ + 5 = 13

9) __ + 8 = 11   10) __ + 3 = 12

11) __ + 9 = 14   12) __ + 4 = 14

Write the missing number to make the sum complete

1) $\_ + 2 = 16$ 2) $\_ + 3 = 17$

3) $\_ + 1 = 17$ 4) $\_ + 1 = 19$

5) $\_ + 2 = 19$ 6) $\_ + 6 = 19$

7) $\_ + 3 = 16$ 8) $\_ + 3 = 18$

9) $\_ + 5 = 20$ 10) $\_ + 7 = 20$

11) $\_ + 8 = 20$ 12) $\_ + 2 = 17$

ADDITION IN ACTION

Write the missing number to make the sum complete

1) _ + 6 = 20   2) _ + 9 = 19

3) _ + 7 = 17   4) _ + 4 = 18

5) _ + 5 = 16   6) _ + 5 = 18

7) _ + 8 = 17   8) _ + 9 = 20

9) _ + 4 = 19   10) _ + 0 = 17

11) _ + 13 = 20   12) _ + 7 = 18

YOU ACED ADDITION!

Excellent work!

SECTION 4: LET'S LEARN SUBTRACTION

SUBTRACTION

Subtraction is when you take one number away from another number

$$4 - 3 = 1$$

In this example, we start with 4 stars and then take 3 away, which leaves us with just 1 star

Let's see a few more examples . . .

LET'S LEARN SUBTRACTION

$$2 - 1 = 1$$

$$4 - 2 = 2$$

$$3 - 1 = 2$$

6 - 3 = 3

5 - 2 = 3

Now your turn ➡

LET'S LEARN
SUBTRACTION

3 - 2 = ☐

2 - 1 = ☐

4 - 2 = ☐

6 - 5 =

5 - 1 =

6 - 3 =

Let's take away the stars

$$5 - 1 = \boxed{}$$

$$3 - 1 = \boxed{}$$

$$4 - 3 = \boxed{}$$

Let's take away the stars

$8 - 2 =$

$6 - 3 =$

$7 - 5 =$

LET'S LEARN SUBTRACTION

Sums can also look like this:

$$7 - 2 =$$

$$9 - 6 =$$

$$6 - 5 =$$

$$5 - 3 =$$

LET'S LEARN SUBTRACTION

Sums can also look like this:

$$8 - 2 =$$

$$9 - 1 =$$

$$4 - 4 =$$

$$5 - 0 =$$

SECTION 5: SUBTRACTION IN ACTION

SUBTRACTION IN ACTION

Count the circles, write down the numbers, solve the sum

1) 3
  − 2
  ____
    1

2) □
  − □
  ____

3) □
  − □
  ____

4) □
  − □
  ____

5) □
  − □
  ____

6) □
  − □
  ____

7) □
  − □
  ____

8) □
  − □
  ____

SUBTRACTION IN ACTION

Count the circles, write down the numbers, solve the sum

1)

2)

3)

4)

5)

6)

7)

8)

SUBTRACTION IN ACTION

Count the circles, write down the numbers, solve the sum

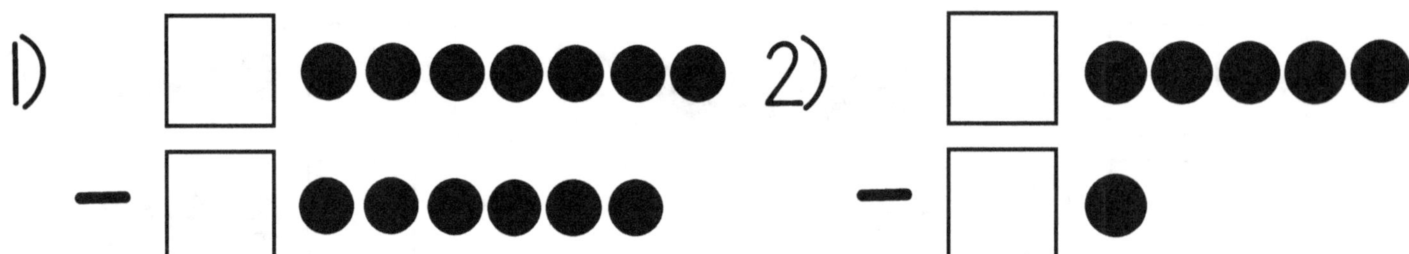

1)

2)

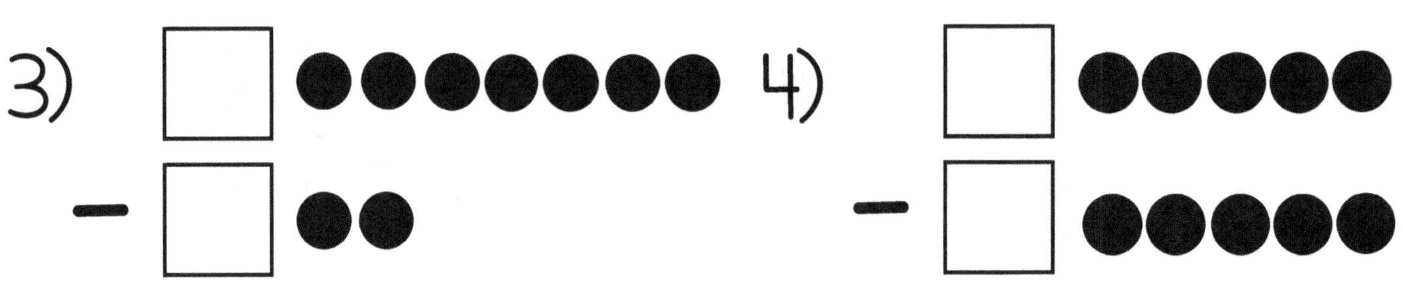

3)

4)

5)

6)

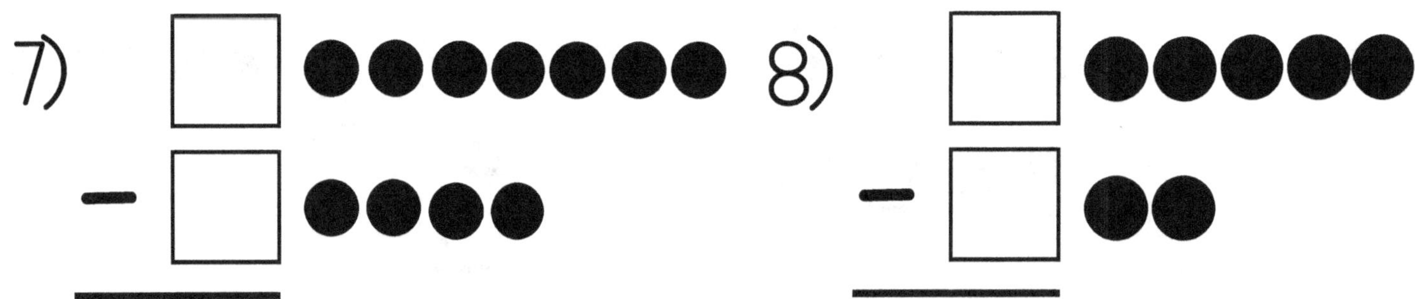

7)

8)

SUBTRACTION IN ACTION

Count the circles, write down the numbers, solve the sum

1)

2)

3)

4)

5)

6)

7)

8)

SUBTRACTION IN ACTION

Count the circles, write down the numbers, solve the sum

1) $\underline{2} - \underline{2} = \underline{0}$

2) $\underline{} - \underline{} = \underline{}$

3) $\underline{} - \underline{} = \underline{}$

4) $\underline{} - \underline{} = \underline{}$

5) $\underline{} - \underline{} = \underline{}$

SUBTRACTION IN ACTION

Count the circles, write down the numbers, solve the sum

1)

___ - ___ = ___

2)

___ - ___ = ___

3)

___ - ___ = ___

4)

___ - ___ = ___

5)

___ - ___ = ___

SUBTRACTION IN ACTION

Count the circles, write down the numbers, solve the sum

1) ●   −   __ − __ = __

2) ●●● ●● − ●●● ●●   __ − __ = __

3) ●●● ●●● − ●●   __ − __ = __

4) ●● ●● − ●● ●●   __ − __ = __

5) ●●● ●●● − ●●● ●●   __ − __ = __

SUBTRACTION IN ACTION

Count the circles, write down the numbers, solve the sum

1) 

_ _ - _ _ = _ _

2)

_ _ - _ _ = _ _

3)

_ _ - _ _ = _ _

4)

_ _ - _ _ = _ _

5)

_ _ - _ _ = _ _

SUBTRACTION IN ACTION

Draw the circles and write the number that solves the sum

1) $6 - 2 = 4$

2) $3 - \underline{} = 0$

3) $6 - \underline{} = 1$

4) $4 - \underline{} = 2$

5) $9 - \underline{} = 2$

SUBTRACTION IN ACTION

Draw the circles and write the number that solves the sum

1)   ⭕⭕⭕ −
     ⭕⭕

$\underline{5} - \underline{} = \underline{2}$

2)   ⭕⭕⭕
     ⭕⭕⭕ −
     ⭕

$\underline{7} - \underline{} = \underline{1}$

3)   ⭕⭕⭕ −
     ⭕⭕

$\underline{5} - \underline{} = \underline{0}$

4)   ⭕⭕⭕
     ⭕⭕⭕ −
     ⭕⭕

$\underline{8} - \underline{} = \underline{3}$

5)   ⭕⭕⭕⭕
     ⭕⭕⭕⭕ −
     ⭕⭕

$\underline{10} - \underline{} = \underline{5}$

SUBTRACTION IN ACTION

Draw the circles and write the number that solves the sum

1) $6 - \_ = 4$

2) $2 - \_ = 1$

3) $9 - \_ = 3$

4) $8 - \_ = 1$

5) $4 - \_ = 3$

SUBTRACTION IN ACTION

Draw the circles and write the number that solves the sum

1) $5 - \_\_ = 1$

2) $3 - \_\_ = 1$

3) $7 - \_\_ = 4$

4) $10 - \_\_ = 2$

5) $10 - \_\_ = 7$

SUBTRACTION IN ACTION

Take one number away from the other to solve the sum

1) $8 - 8 = 0$

2) $9 - 4 =$

3) $7 - 2 =$

4) $4 - 2 =$

5) $5 - 1 =$

6) $6 - 1 =$

7) $5 - 2 =$

8) $5 - 4 =$

9) $6 - 3 =$

10) $6 - 4 =$

11) $7 - 6 =$

12) $3 - 3 =$

Take one number away from the other to solve the sum

1) $1 - 0 =$

2) $4 - 0 =$

3) $9 - 0 =$

4) $7 - 3 =$

5) $9 - 5 =$

6) $7 - 4 =$

7) $5 - 5 =$

8) $8 - 3 =$

9) $8 - 4 =$

10) $8 - 7 =$

11) $9 - 8 =$

12) $7 - 7 =$

SUBTRACTION IN ACTION

Take one number away from the other to solve the sum

1) 12 − 5 =

2) 12 − 4 =

3) 11 − 3 =

4) 15 − 6 =

5) 14 − 9 =

6) 12 − 8 =

7) 11 − 4 =

8) 13 − 9 =

9) 10 − 4 =

10) 12 − 6 =

11) 13 − 1 =

12) 15 − 8 =

Take one number away from the other to solve the sum

1) $12 - 2 =$

2) $14 - 7 =$

3) $17 - 3 =$

4) $15 - 3 =$

5) $13 - 4 =$

6) $19 - 0 =$

7) $17 - 2 =$

8) $16 - 3 =$

9) $14 - 5 =$

10) $19 - 8 =$

11) $20 - 0 =$

12) $12 - 3 =$

SUBTRACTION IN ACTION

Write the missing number to make the sum complete

1) $7 - \_ = 3$

2) $6 - \_ = 2$

3) $9 - \_ = 1$

4) $7 - \_ = 1$

5) $9 - \_ = 6$

6) $9 - \_ = 2$

7) $8 - \_ = 3$

8) $6 - \_ = 3$

9) $10 - \_ = 7$

10) $10 - \_ = 5$

11) $7 - \_ = 2$

12) $10 - \_ = 8$

SUBTRACTION IN ACTION

Write the missing number to make the sum complete

1) 11 - __ = 7   2) 10 - __ = 6

3) 10 - __ = 4   4) 11 - __ = 2

5) 14 - __ = 11   6) 12 - __ = 7

7) 13 - __ = 5   8) 12 - __ = 6

9) 12 - __ = 11   10) 11 - __ = 3

11) 14 - __ = 1   12) 14 - __ = 5

SUBTRACTION IN ACTION

Write the missing number to make the sum complete

1) 17 - __ = 3   2) 16 - __ = 2

3) 19 - __ = 1   4) 17 - __ = 1

5) 19 - __ = 6   6) 19 - __ = 2

7) 18 - __ = 8   8) 16 - __ = 3

9) 19 - __ = 7   10) 20 - __ = 7

11) 17 - __ = 6   12) 20 - __ = 8

SUBTRACTION IN ACTION

Write the missing number to make the sum complete

1) 19 - __ = 9   2) 20 - __ = 6

3) 18 - __ = 4   4) 17 - __ = 7

5) 18 - __ = 5   6) 16 - __ = 9

7) 20 - __ = 11   8) 17 - __ = 8

9) 17 - __ = 2   10) 19 - __ = 5

11) 18 - __ = 3   12) 20 - __ = 16

WELL DONE!

Certificate of Achievement

TeachTime certifies that:

____

is simply brilliant at adding & subtracting

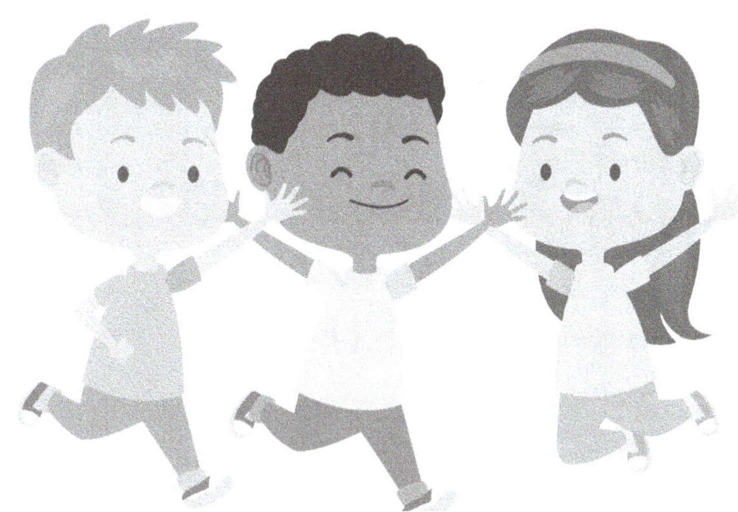

ALSO FROM TEACHTIME
Available on Amazon

THE IDEAL
BOOK TO
BEGIN
WRITING

MASTER
CURSIVE
WRITING
EASILY

ALL THE SIGHT
WORDS YOUR
CHILD MUST
KNOW

www.ingramcontent.com/pod-product-compliance
Lightning Source LLC
Chambersburg PA
CBHW080304030726
47593CB00009B/2621